Double Your Business

DOUBLE YOUR BUSINESS

THE ENTREPRENEUR'S GUIDE

to Double Your Profits
Without Doubling Your Hours
So That You Can Actually Enjoy Your Life

CASSIE PARKS

NEW YORK

NASHVILLE • MELBOURNE • VANCOUVER

Double Your Business

The Entrepreneur's Guide to Double Your Profits Without Doubling Your Hours so You Can Actually Enjoy Your Life

© 2017 Cassie Parks

Published in New York, New York, by Morgan James Publishing in partnership with Difference Press. Morgan James is a trademark of Morgan James, LLC.
www.MorganJamesPublishing.com

The Morgan James Speakers Group can bring authors to your live event. For more information or to book an event visit The Morgan James Speakers Group at www.TheMorganJamesSpeakersGroup.com.

ISBN 9781683504269 paperback
ISBN 9781683504276 eBook
Library of Congress Control Number: 2017901205

Cover Design by:
Rachel Lopez
www.r2cdesign.com

Interior Design by:
Chris Treccani
www.3dogdesign.net

In an effort to support local communities, raise awareness and funds, Morgan James Publishing donates a percentage of all book sales for the life of each book to Habitat for Humanity Peninsula and Greater Williamsburg.

Get involved today! Visit
www.MorganJamesBuilds.com

Dedication

To Angela. Thank you for being a lighthouse.

Table of Contents

Chapter 1

You want to double your business. Who doesn't, right?

Then you could move into the house you've been dreaming about, the one in that great neighborhood with your favorite coffee shop and those homes that instantly transport you back in time with their character and charm. You definitely want to double your business, but what you *really* want is that house–and you just can't get there with the way things are now.

Take Kerri. Kerri started in real estate when she was 25 because she wanted to pick her own hours and to be in charge of how she made money. She didn't want to sit behind a desk 9-5 waiting for a promotion to make the kind of income she wanted.

This is how a typical day in her life looks and feels now, three years later:

Kerri walks into the coffee shop this morning and orders a double latte. For the last three weeks, she has been up late working on her laptop in bed. She yawns as she reaches for the coffee. Back in the car, she starts driving to her closing. It's 7 a.m., and as she sits in traffic, she wonders how she could ever take on more than she is already doing. She's got two closings this morning, then she has to drive back to her office to do paperwork, and then she'll probably be showing houses until late at night.

When the light turns green, she thinks back to her first closing. She remembers getting that check and it being the greatest thing ever. She knew she could make this business work. After all, it's just houses, right? That first check was bigger than most of her friends were making going in every day 9-5 for two weeks. It was such a great feeling!

The next one was a little harder to come by, but it worked out–and sure enough, she started selling more and more houses and listings started coming her way. She was working hard, but it came naturally–it was just reaching out and talking to people she knew. Everything was awesome. That first year was great.

When she stops at the red light, she thinks about the last two years. She's not sure what happened, but it has stopped being as fun as it was. Is it because she's been doing it for over three years now? Or is it because it seems to be costing her more money to make more money, and she's not sure how she can keep going at this pace? How can she work harder and still be happy when her time is completely eaten up by working?

At 28, things are mostly good in Kerri's life, though it's different than she thought it would be. She has a great husband, and they live in a nice house. It's not her dream house, but it's nicer than most of her friends have. But she really wants to move to an old house near downtown. She longs to buy one and save it before someone comes along and demolishes it, like the last two houses she fell in love with.

When the light turns green, Kerri thinks about the money. She really wants to make more money, but the current plan she is working is sucking the life out of her. She wonders what it would be like to live on $20,000 less a year. By the time she hits the next red light, she decides that's not going to work.

She presses the pedal when the light turns green and she thinks about all the advice she has gotten in the last six months. Her income has increased, but she's got a long list of things to do every day, she's exhausted, and she's not sure if the trade-off is worth it. It seems like it's costing her a lot more time to make relatively small gains.

She pulls into the parking lot, and shuts off the car. She thinks, "Okay, I've got about ten minutes here to figure this out."

Truth is, she has been trying to figure this out for three months. She invested in a marketing plan because everybody told her it was necessary in order to expand her business, and it felt like the right thing to do. No one told her she was going to have to put in three times as much work. The clients she's attracting are shopping at a much lower price point then the ones last year, even though the market is up 5%. The math just doesn't seem right, but she's out of time to figure it out and has to go inside. She grabs her bag, gets out, and waits until the lights flash as she walks away from her 328i.

Kerri, like most people, has been sold the story that you have to "sacrifice now to get what you want later." That's what you're supposed to do, right? Be miserable now so that someday you will meet your goals? Kerri is starting to question the validity of that, and perhaps you are, too.

Do you really have to give up everything now to get what you want later? Do you really have to be exhausted and frustrated and work what feels like every hour of the day to get where you want to go? Isn't there an easier way?

Kerri, like most real estate agents and business owners, has been sold the myth that you have to set a goal, devise a plan to get there, and then work really, really hard to achieve it. She's done all the things she's been told to do. She is working long hours. She has paid more to market her business than ever before.

And, even with her great husband and nice house, she is more miserable than ever before.

Maybe you feel like Kerri. Over the last three years, you've made good money in your business. It's been fun, but about six months ago, you started trying to figure out how to double your income. You have looked up articles. You have talked to people you consider to be good mentors and advisors. You've thought about hiring a coach, but are no longer sure what the next best thing is to do. There are about five ways you have learned that *might* work to double your business, but if you are honest with yourself, none of them feels good. They all seem to require more of you than you feel you have to give.

You know how to work hard, and you're good at it, you always have been. But there comes a point where it feels like you can't work any harder because there are literally only 24 hours in a day, and you have a husband, you have girlfriends, and you'd like to be able to see your parents every couple weeks.

You want to double your business, but you cannot double your hours to do so. There has to be a better way, right?

I understand how you feel. Not that long ago, I felt the same way. I quit my corporate job to be a coach so that I could set my own hours and do what I love without giving up my ability to travel and go lay in the park reading a romance novel in the middle of the day on a Wednesday. After all, being in charge of my schedule and deciding how much I wanted to work were the very reasons I left that corporate gig. I did not want to give that freedom up–but I still wanted to make more money.

Maybe you feel like I did, that the choice before you is to double your business and give up your life, or stay where you are, keep about the same hours, and give up on some of your dreams. Like that house. The house that is so beautiful, it makes you swoon just to think of driving up the street shaded by the big trees on both sides. That is the dream you would have to give up. You are not willing to do that, either. You probably feel stuck.

I felt like it was time to get serious and make some more money. The problem was, I felt like I was already working a lot. How many more hours was I going to have to work to double or triple my income? If I wanted to double my income, wasn't I was going to have to double my hours? That didn't feel good–or possible.

The other part that didn't feel good was that I didn't actually know *how* to double my business. Yes, I had learned lots of things over the years, and more marketing seemed like the agreed-upon option, but I didn't know how to increase my efforts without tapping out my market.

A lot of people were telling me a lot of strategies, but I didn't know if they would actually work for my business and my goals. The traditional path says work harder, market more, just keep grinding away. But, like you, I didn't know if I wanted to sacrifice my remaining free time–or even have a clear idea of what would be effective about doing so.

The traditional way says to stand where you are and look toward the future. Set your goal and start working towards it. That feels like a lot of hard work, sacrifice, and guessing, but it's probably the only path you can see right now. It's where I was, and where many of my clients find themselves when they start working with me.

Is there a better, easier way? Yes, and I've found it.

It works like this: set your income intention, figure out who that person who is making that much money (your future self), and how she is living her life. Then step into being her as much as possible, and watch as what you want starts to happen around you. Do you still have to work? Yes, you still have to do the things you do in your business, but this way allows you to grow quickly and easily without the grind of putting in more hours or the despair of giving up on your dreams.

I am going to explain this like I would explain it to Kerri. In real estate, there are two ways to make the same amount of money. You can sell four $200,000 homes, or you can sell one $800,000 home. You have to do all the paperwork, showings, inspections, closings, and all the other steps for each house, which means you have to do it four times for the $200,000 properties and only once for the $800,000 home. You make the same, but one is a lot easier. Less work, same money.

What if your whole business could be like the one $800,000 sale instead of the four $200,000 sales? Do you think you would have the time to double your business if it meant selling one more house instead of four?

You might be thinking, "Yes, I want to do that, but how?"

If Kerri was being lead the traditional way, someone would probably tell her to send a bunch of marketing material to $800,000 neighborhoods (because that seems like the smart thing to do). The problem is that 1) she doesn't know if that is going to work, and 2) she feels like it's a big investment with no guarantee of paying off with more listings.

She could also cold call old listings in that neighborhood, and has probably been told to do that several times. But she has heard horror stories from her clients about getting ten cold calls from different agents and how annoying it is, so that feels out of integrity. Kerri doesn't want to be that person.

How about you? Do you feel the same?

You have the same traditional marketing options in front of you, but they seem hard and, quite frankly, unpalatable. You started your own business so you could be who you wanted to be, make money, and enjoy your life in the process. You built your business just by talking to people and doing a great job. You built it while enjoying your life, and you really liked that. Now, you feel stuck because it doesn't seem like doing the same things that made you successful in the beginning are going to make you the money you really want to be making.

My client Maggie wasn't a real estate agent, but she was working a job she hated. In fact, she describes it as toxic. During her 60 days working with me, she was offered a job that paid $20,000 more than she was making at the toxic job and allowed her the time and space to do the other things she loves to do. I'm telling you this story because I want you to know it is possible to make more money while enjoying your life more. Making more money does not have to cost you all your free time and feel draining.

In order to make more, work less, and love your life even more, you just have to be open to doing it the non-traditional way. If you choose to keep following me through the next pages, I will teach you the process I used to double my business more than once, and that allows me to take Wednesdays off, travel the world (I am writing this book from a villa in Tuscany), and live in the home of my dreams. (The one I secretly dreamed of and never thought would be a possibility for me.)

I understand where you are at. Your brain is telling you to market more, to do more. That was where my client Jill was when she was trying to sell her first coaching program. Jill had sold ten clients in ten weeks, but wanted to sell more. She thought for sure that what she needed to do was more marketing. She wanted to have sold 20 entries into her program by the time we started working together, but that wasn't happening. She was frustrated, and wasn't sure how she could work any harder. She also didn't know how to market differently.

She was doing what she had been told, but it wasn't working.

Jill and I worked closely together for three days. On the fourth day, she sold another five entries into her program by sending out one email. Although Jill had sent out lots of emails before we worked together, this time around, she opened up to the idea of it simply being easier to get clients–and then it was. Within ten days of attending my workshop, she had sold an additional ten spots, which means she doubled her business in the ten days after we worked together.

Jill is not more special than you. She doesn't know more. She simply stepped into the version of herself who makes more money doing what she loves, while fully enjoying the life she has built. In the next chapter, I will tell you the steps I took Jill through that helped her transform herself into the business owner she longed to be.

I have another client, Jennifer, who does sales for her business. The month after we worked together, she sold double what she had the month before–and she didn't work any harder. She, too, felt like she was at a standstill. She knew there had to be a different way, one that didn't require her to work around the clock or create a whole new way of doing business that didn't feel good.

Here is the secret to Jill and Jennifer doubling their business in a short time: we were able to get them clear about what it looks like to make the money they wanted to be making, and still enjoy their life. From that place, the path appeared quickly and easily. I will tell you step by step how to do this later in the book.

If you were able to double your business in the next year, without stressing or overworking, how would that feel? What would be different in your life? What is the first thing you would do with the money?

I always love talking about how great it will be when you double your business. But it's also important to consider what *putting off* doubling your business can cost you. For example, every month I might have put off doubling my business would have cost me $12,500, because that is how much more a month I am making at this point in my business. Putting it off for three months would have cost me $37,500. If I would have put it off for six months, it would have cost me $75,000. That's a 20% down payment on a great house! Five years from now, that's three quarters of a million dollars!

If you had $750,000 five years from now, what would be different? Where would you be living? What would you be doing? Where would you be taking your next vacation?

What is the cost of putting off making just two more sales a month? For Kerri, it is around $20,000 a month. What does your life look like a year from now when you have made an additional $240,000? What would you be doing differently today if you had that amount in your checking account? That's enough to put a down payment on a million-dollar house. Take a few minutes and figure it out for yourself. What is the financial cost of not doubling your business in the next year? What will that keep you from having, being, or doing that is really important to you?

It's not just the financial cost of what isn't in your pocket that matters. Inflation and the market are factors, too. In Denver, the real estate market keeps rising, so every month Kerri does not invest in her dream house, that house probably costs $10,000 more than it did the month before. Kerri wants a million-dollar home just outside of downtown Denver that she can restore. The cost of putting off her dream is not just what her business would make, it's also another $120,000 a year.

Then there is the emotional cost of putting off living a life you really love. What are you putting off because you are trying to double your business? What is the emotional cost of working harder and more hours than you want to be? These are the costs we don't always see. It could be the extra stress of not having the amount in savings that makes you feel comfortable. It could be not getting to experience the joy of living in the neighborhood you desire. It could be the turmoil you constantly feel wondering if it would be better to just go get a 9-5 job. It might even be the frustration of not feeling as successful as you want to feel. How are those feelings having an effect on your everyday life?

Take a minute to think about what it is costing you *not* to double your business, both financially and emotionally. These things have probably been rolling around in your head for a while, you just haven't looked at the full list or verbalized it. Write down the cost so that you can see it. It will feel good to get it out of your head, and, once you do, you can start to shift your energy.

Imagine what it would feel like if you doubled your business? What would your bank account would look like? Maybe you have started to do this, but have become overwhelmed because the only path you know is to sacrifice now in order to get what you want later. Then you start thinking, "What if I give up everything now and I still don't get there?"

Follow me through the next pages and I will show you how living as close to your dream life as you can right now can double your business even faster–because you are not sacrificing all your time, energy, and happiness along the way.

I think there are two ways to do anything: the quick slow way, and the slow quick way. Think of it in terms of dieting. When someone diets to lose a 100 pounds, they can do it really quickly if they change everything they are doing. But when they get off the diet, they usually gain the weight right back. That is the quick slow way because it came off quickly, but it's slow because they are going to have to do more work to get to where they want to be. If, instead, they changed their life to be more like the life of the person who is 100 pounds lighter, it would take longer. It's the slow quick way because it's slower than a quick-fix diet, but it's going to get them where they want to be much quicker because they are not going to gain the weight back.

For you, the quick slow way is doing things like more marketing, cold calling, working tons of hours, and sacrificing your life now to get results later. You can absolutely double your business this way, but you aren't likely to maintain your efforts because all that sacrifice doesn't feel good and you are likely to want your old life back.

If you learn the slow, quick way, we can change your life to mirror that of the life you have with double your income. You can create a life that feels good and doubles your business. In the end, it will be the quickest path— because not only is it sustainable, it's enjoyable.

You have probably felt for a while like there is no good option to double your business and feel good. If you read this book and follow my suggestions, you will see that option you have been looking for appear. And—this is important—the option that will work best for you is unique to you.

In the next pages, I am going to show you the way. I will walk you step by step through the process I used and have used with many of my clients to help them double their business and fall more in love with their life. I am also going to show you where you might get stuck so you know how to navigate out of these places. It does not have to be as hard as you have been told, and you do not have to sacrifice all your time and energy to double your business.

I love reading books, but I get more out of one-on-one interaction. As you read this book, if you find yourself loving the process but are getting stuck, I am always happy to go deeper with you. You can go to http://www.imreadytodoublemybusiness. com *and schedule a call with me.*

Chapter 2

Looks like you are all in for doubling your business because you made it to chapter 2! I am so happy you are here. In chapter 1, we talked about the quick, slow way and the slow, quick way. Just because I call it the slow, quick way doesn't mean it has to be a snail's pace. You saw with Jill and Jennifer that their results were almost instantaneous. That is totally possible for you– and, in fact, is more often the norm for my clients.

The reason the slow, quick way works is that you are setting yourself up for sustainable growth that FEELS good to you. You are laying the groundwork first, and then going into action. Conversely, in the quick, slow way, you are diving head-first into things you are hoping will work. It's the quick, slow way because often those things don't work, and you have to keep reworking the system and trying something new.

With the slow, quick way, you get to have the life you want now and double your business. The key is to get completely clear about what your life is going to look like when you have doubled your business. We are going to set an income intention, and then analyze the life you will have when that intention comes true. Remember I talked about putting yourself in the future and looking back?

Traditionally, you stand where you are, set a goal, and then try to work your way there. The process I am going to teach you is going to be very different. If you want to double your business without sacrificing everything, you are going to love it.

The intention of doubling my business without having to work more was the reason I put this process in place. I knew there had to be a way to double my income without doubling my hours. Before working this process, I took all kinds of courses and tried different marketing techniques, but in the back of my mind I knew there was something I was missing, even though I couldn't see it yet. In my case, my best path to easily doubling my business showed up via a mentor who opened my eyes and taught me the things I had never been taught.

I don't know exactly what the most efficient path, the means to get you where you want to go, to doubling your business without doubling your hours, will look like for you in particular. The way forward that appears for everyone is unique and different, and is just right for them. It shows up when you go through the process and get clear about every part of the life you desire to be living. When you are clear about what your future life looks like, exactly what you need to get there will appear.

It might be a mentor that can teach you what you have been missing, like in my case. Or in the case of Kerri, it might be a magical client that is an endless referral source. It might be being in the right place at the right time where you get to be the agent for an entire new build project. You might be like my client Jill, and all of a sudden the right words flow out of you that invite the sales you have been waiting on. She was inspired the day after we finished our work to send out an email. From that one email, she sold five spots in her coaching program. You could also be like Jennifer and just by getting clear, sales start happening easier without extra work.

Whatever it is, it will be the perfect thing for you. It will also be the quickest and easiest path to get you where you want to be. Every client is unique, and this process looks different for each of them. Every time, the path to their dream life appears. I have used this process to double my business three times, and each time the path has looked different. I am so excited to share it with you because each time my business doubles, the time it takes to double decreases by half and I am not working more hours to do it.

Set an Income Intention

The first thing we are going to talk about is how a goal is different than an intention. We are taught to set goals and to make them specific, measurable, realistic, and time-related. The problem with that is that goals lack the depth and clarity needed to allow your easy path to appear. Making them realistic keeps you in a bubble that really isn't big enough for you to grow into them. When you get focused on measuring them and putting a deadline on them, you feel rushed—and it's almost inevitable that you will pick the quick, slow way because of that. Setting a goal breeds the quick, slow way. I will show you how setting an intention will open up the process and allow your business to grow faster without more work.

Create Your Future Budget

Once you have your income intention, you will create your future budget. Creating your future budget is important because your brain resists what it cannot conceive. If you set a big income intention, but you have no idea how that money is going to be spent, it's harder to create the path to it. Your brain will constantly be questioning why you are trying to get there. Knowing how your money is going to be allocated gets your brain to be with you in this process instead of against you.

Analyze Your Budget

Analyzing your budget is the next step. Once you have that analysis, you can look at it for clues about who you are in your future life. It is common to think that you're going to be exactly the same, but have more money. When you look at your budget, you will realize that is not true, and in fact, knowing how you are going to be different is a key part of the process. If you do not know who you are going to be, you cannot step into that person, and stepping into that person, your future self, is the key to not having to give up your life in order to double your business.

Meet Your Future Self

When people talk about their future self, most of their observations are made by the present self looking forward and guessing. The problem with that is that you don't know for sure who your future self is, and you are not in touch enough to see how she will be different. It's the differences that are the keys to unlocking the quick and easy path. In the next step of the process, meeting your future self, I will teach you a process for taking your budget and getting familiar with who your future self actually is.

Mirror Your Future Life

After we have been introduced to your future self, you will take what you know and start to mirror your future life with it. Most people think their dream life is light years away. That's because they feel like they have to get there. They want so much to be there that they miss what is right in front of them. My clients always tell me, "Wow. So much of the future I want is already here." That is most people's experience. They just have not been able to see it. You will learn how to appreciate what already exists in your life, and look for ways you can bring what is not yet in your current life into existence now. This way you will get to experience as much of your future life now as possible. Experiencing more of your future now will take away the desperate need to "get there." When that happens, what you desire–like doubling your business–comes about quickly and easily. Business is drawn to you, instead of you working so hard to get it.

Step into Your Future

Once you have mirrored your current life as close to your future life as possible, you will learn how to tap into the experiences that you know you will be having in your future life. You will learn to take big steps into your future life. This will expand your awareness to include the experiences you will be having in your future life. The physical experience is an important part of the process. It's a step many people do not know how to do, and it helps get your brain on board.

Experiencing Your Future

Once you have gone through all these steps, you will start to notice events happening in your life that match your future life. It's important to take note of these. Savor the moments. Allow them to be a channel to get to know your future self on a deeper level.

Go Deeper

Most people have done some part of what I have described above. The problem is, most people do not go deep enough. Doing one part without the whole process leaves you with a hole in your knowledge and understanding of your future self. This makes it harder for the path to doubling your business to appear. The key is to continue meeting your future self, mirroring her life, and stepping into her experiences so that you experience more and more of your future self. This process continues and gets deeper every time.

The reason this process works is that your future self starts to guide you. You know when you have the intuition to call someone out of the blue and that leads to a sale? Or you just happen to stop at a random store and run into someone that makes a difference in your business? Those things start to happen so much faster, and they become more and more powerful. At the end of the book, I will tell you the story of how one client can actually double your business–and it happens by being connected to the future you desire and following your intuition and inspiration, rather than coming up with the perfect tag line for your marketing copy.

Let's get started!

Chapter 3

Goals vs. Intentions

When I ask my clients what they want their income to be, they usually come up with a number a couple different ways. One way is to add the amount that something they have been wanting to do would cost to their current income. So if they are making $5,000 a month and they want to go on a $2,000 vacation, they will say $7,000. This is because this is the information they have to work with. I am living off $5,000, but I don't have enough for a vacation, so I would like to make $7,000. It makes sense logically, especially because no one ever told you how to set a proper income intention.

The other answer I get is one that seems reasonable, but doesn't feel like asking too much. It's something that is more than they are making, but that won't really make an impact on their lifestyle.

The reason for this is that the traditional way to increase your income is to set a goal that is just above where you are now and that feels comfortable, and then come up with a plan to get there. But there is so little space in the goal that there isn't room to grow. You have probably heard before that you have to grow into the next level of your income. You do. However, it's actually easier to grow a lot than a little. It can be hard to find a way to grow into a 10% increase, but if your intention is a 100% or even 1000% increase, there is lots more room to grow and it will actually be easier.

I am going to talk about growing in terms of a bubble. In some industries, like real estate, bubbles burst because they get too big. I am not talking about that kind of bubble. I am talking about the bubble you are living in, like a goldfish lives in its bowl. In the wild, goldfish grow to the size that will allow them to survive in their environment and not take up too many resources. There are hormones that regulate this. When they are kept as pets, they don't get very big, but when they are in the ocean, they continue to grow and grow as long as their environment will support that growth.

Your bubble is like the goldfish's bowl. And the size of your bubble is determined by your goals and dreams. You will grow, not physically like the goldfish, but mentally, emotionally, and spiritually, to the size of your bubble. The bigger your goals and dreams, the more space you have to grow into the size of your bubble. The space you have to grow into is the space between where you are now and where you are when you have doubled your business. If you set an income intention just above where you are now, you aren't expanding your bubble very much—so there won't be room for a lot of growth. If you are going to double your business, however, you need more space to grow, mentally, emotionally, and, possibly, spiritually. By setting that big income intention, you create that space to grow, because setting the intention expands your bubble.

When you first started your business, your bubble seemed big because you hadn't yet grown into it. You had what seemed, at the time, like a big goal and dream. There was a big space between where you were and where you wanted to be. When you are a business owner, two main things make up the space in your bubble: your business knowledge, and your capacity for allowing money into your life. When you first started your business, most of the space in your bubble was probably created because of your lack of business knowledge. You likely hadn't run a business before, and there was lots to learn and lots of room for growth.

Even though you had to grow as a business owner, you may or may not have had to expand your money capacity much. If you knew lots of people making $50,000, you probably grew up thinking $50,000 was totally doable. When you started your business, you could likely easily figure out how to make $50,000 a year. Your brain could go there. It could figure out the path. Thinking back to Kerri: when she got started in real estate, she probably figured out all she had to do was sell six $300,000 homes a year.

Take a minute to think about how much of your life you thought you would make $50,000. It was probably a fair amount. As I said earlier, you had to grow in terms of business knowledge but probably not as much, if any, in terms of money capacity. This is part of the reason you feel stuck, now that you are trying to increase your income from $50,000 to $100,000. You are probably doing the same things you did to take your income from $0-$50,000.

The problem is, you are only focused on growing your business knowledge instead of both your business knowledge and money capacity. This probably hasn't been working super well because you didn't expand your bubble by setting a big enough income intention. Now it's time to grow your money capacity while simultaneously growing your business capacity. You may find you actually need to focus more on your money capacity than your business knowledge at this point. That will become clear as you go through the steps in this process.

By setting an income intention that creates a big bubble, you are creating a bubble that will require you to grow your money capacity, business knowledge, and lifestyle capacity all at once. When you have a bubble that has the space to grow these together, you will be able to quickly and easily grow your business to the next level with a lot less work.

Traditionally, people will say to keep growing in order to get your income to a high level. This is the harder way, because you're actually trying to grow out of your bubble instead of creating a new, bigger one by setting an income intention. When you set a bigger income intention, you are naturally going to expand your bubble. The next steps I will teach you in the process will show you where and how you need to grow and encompass business, money, and lifestyle expansion instead of you just guessing how to grow and trying to make your next income goal happen.

Set an Income Intention

The first step in this process is to set an income intention.

The reason I use the word "intention" is because the definition is "a determination to act." A goal on the other hand, is defined as "the object of a person's ambition or effort; an aim or desired result."

When you have a goal, by definition it's a desire, something you're aiming for. This is different from an intention, because an intention isn't a result, it's a determination to act. Basically, when you set a goal you are aiming for something. If you have good aim, you'll get there. If your aim is bad, you probably won't. When you set a goal, you are aiming for a target, but you are trying to line up with the target beforehand. You are setting up the trajectory of your arrow, if you will, by creating a marketing plan, allocating more funds to your marketing budget, committing to going to more networking events. All of these types of activities are "aiming" activities, but you don't know how good your aim is until you pull back and let go.

The target is also small. Imagine standing with a bow and arrow. Your arrow is at most a quarter inch in diameter, no bigger than a nickel for sure. Then you are going to aim for something the size of the mouth of your favorite coffee mug? If you have been setting goals and not meeting them, this is part of the reason. You have to make a best estimation of where to aim and then let go, hoping you lined it up good enough to hit your mark.

The other thing about a goal is that it is the "object of a person's ambition." It's an object, not a way of being. There is only one destination: the middle of the target. Think of the circle in the middle of the target as the goal. You have to get the goal in order to have the things in the outer rings. If you miss and just hit the outer ring, in terms of your goals, you have actually failed.

When you set an intention, everything within you starts to move in action toward your goal. You literally start taking steps toward the goal instead of just pulling back your arrow and shooting. You actually *become* the arrow, and you determine your own direction—as opposed to just letting go and hoping your aim was on target. When you set an intention, everything in you starts moving in the direction of that intention, which means you are not putting off your life to get there. You are creating your life as you go, and that makes getting there easier. The other great thing about having an intention is that you get to aim at the whole target. When you get to any place on the target, it means you are closer to your goal rather than having failed to get to your goal. I will talk more about this in upcoming chapters. Understanding the basic difference between an income goal and an intention is important to understand before ever setting an intention or a goal, because it determines how you are going to proceed through the process.

As I mentioned earlier, people generally set an income goal based on what they are making, plus extra to cover the current thing, like a vacation or a new car. Or they choose a modest number they would be happy with. In either case, it's just enough to be more than what they have now, without significantly impacting their lifestyle. This keeps your bubble small.

If you keep your income intention small, you keep your bubble small. Like the goldfish and her bowl, you only grow big enough for your bubble. If you wanted to let a pet goldfish grow, you would get her a bigger home. In order for you to grow, you have to set a bigger income intention that expands your bubble.

When I sat down to do this with my client Alicia, who was just starting her business, she derived her income goal based on a modest number she thought she would be happy with. In her words: "I would be happy just to make $5,000." That was less than she had made in her previous job, but she felt guilty asking for more than that because she did not know what she would do with the money.

This is another reason people do not set big enough income intentions. Their brains cannot conceive what they would do with that money. One reason for that is that they are trying to picture it from where they are now. If you are paying your bills and doing okay now, your brain has a hard time figuring out what you would do with all that money– which is why, after you set your income intention, you are going to figure out exactly what to do with that money. I will talk more about that later in this chapter.

Your income intention is important, and it is best when it comes from a clear place inside you rather than outside you. Often people set their income intention based on external factors. What are other people doing? What do other people think my income should be? What would a successful person say? How do I pick a number people won't judge me for? What would my mentor do? What is a number I think I can make happen? None of these ways come from inside you. When they do not come from inside you, they are not connected to your future self and that makes it harder to make the number a reality, whether it's bigger or smaller than the one that comes from your inner knowing.

Now that you know why it's important to set an income intention and why it can be hard, let's talk about how to get the number. This is going to be easier than you think, and you will want to trust the process fully. Pull out your cell phone and set the timer for 10 seconds. Next you are going to hit start, close your eyes, and let your income intention come to you. Ready, set, go.

What was the number that first popped into your head? Write it down. It's okay to admit it. It will likely be a little bit scary. It is probably different then you thought it would be. This is because this is coming from your knowing and your future self rather than your smart girl brain who would have done lots of calculations and had lots of filters.

Write down the number. This way, you will remember and have it in front of you as we go through the process. If the number seems scary, it's ok. It's scary because you do not know how you are going to get there. It's likely too big for your brain to figure out in this moment, and that is ok. One of the keys to this process is having intentions that are so big, your smart girl brain has to shut off. When you turn off the thinking part of your brain, we can access the knowing part of your brain. The knowing part of your brain is what will lead you quickest and easiest to the place you desire to be.

This is a great exercise to do with a friend. Have them be in charge of the 10-second timer, and have them make you say the number immediately when it comes up. If you have a coach, ask them to guide you through this exercise.

Here are some things that happen when you do this on your own: You will start to think and ask yourself questions like, "I wonder if she meant before taxes or after taxes." You will think, "That number is too big." Then you will try and think your way through manipulating the number.

You might also wonder is it monthly or annually. While I said annually, your brain will still wonder when you sit down to do it, because it's a way to try and think through the number. This is a moment when you really want to get quiet and let your soul speak. Then you want to honor that sacred conversation by listening and not trying to change the answer to be what you think it should be.

How do I know you might want to change the answer? When I am doing this with a client, they always want to back off and change it once they have said it out loud. It feels scary and uncomfortable, because you just created a big huge bubble to grow into. There is so much space that your body, mind, and spirit feel a little lost and a little scared. If you feel this way, it is actually a good thing. It means you have just created a new bubble, and that is very exciting. The first time I did this exercise, it scared me, too, because I could see no way I would get to that number, which was $500,000. Honor your number. It is a sacred part of you.

Doing this alone can be scarier. When you get really quiet and allow the number to come up from your future self, it is often big and, quite frankly, can be overwhelming to think about. After you do this exercise, take a deep breath and then make a conscious choice about whether you are going to move forward with that number. The important thing to remember is that it is always a choice. When you make a conscious choice, no matter what it is, your chances of success greatly increase. It really is ok to say, "No, that is too big and too scary, and I'm going to put this book down right now." The worst thing you can do in this moment is to adjust the number you received to something that feels comfortable. I am being very honest with you: if you change the number, you are unlikely to experience success with this process.

One of the bravest things you are going to do is own that number and follow me through the next pages. My clients will often say right after this exercise, "I don't know what I am going to do with that money." What I find is that all the things they are going to do with that money are often tucked inside the dreams they are too afraid to admit yet. I also find that once we go through the process, they realize that is the exact life they want to be living.

Why is it so hard to ask for what we want? The biggest reason is that your brain feels its job is to keep you safe. And what doesn't feel safe, according to your brain, is to allow you to dream about something it cannot conceive of a path toward. Your brain is actually doing its job, but I would say that it's not its most helpful function when it comes to setting intentions, and once you understand that, it is so much easier to work around it. The good news is, you have already taken the first step to making it easier by being honest about the number that turns off the part of your brain that wants to figure out how you are going to do this.

The other reason asking for what you want feels hard is that you haven't been taught to set an intention in which your whole body, mind, and spirit are going to go all in on. You have been taught to set a goal from the smart, logical part of your brain, and then use that same part of your brain to come up with a plan to get there. When you create a plan, you have to pick one way. In other words, you are going to sell x number of houses at x price to meet your goal. That breaks down to x number of people you need to contact, and x number of marketing pieces you need to send. The problem with this method is that there are lots of paths to the same number. When you set a goal and then a path, you are limiting yourself to that path and closing off any other opportunities to allow it to happen quicker and easier. Your brain goes on a mission, and it is going to keep you on that one course. It's not going to look for backroads or shortcuts that will be faster in traffic or take you by fun sights.

As I mentioned earlier, the first time I did this exercise, the number that came to me was $500,000. The most I had made in my life was $96,000, and I was making about $1000 a month at that point in my coaching practice. Honestly, it freaked me out a little bit. I didn't know how I was ever going to make that much money. Also, my last marketing strategy, which took me a few months to execute, hadn't worked. However, I knew that number came from inside. I knew it came from my future self, so I made the decision to own it.

Equally importantly, I added some juiciness to the intention because the one thing I was clear about was that I was going to feel good while doing it. So in that moment, I set the intention to not just make $500,000 a year, but to make it from my bed and my balcony. I added my bed and my balcony because I loved my balcony, and I was living in a studio apartment, so I often sat on my bed and worked. That felt good and fun, and it was so big that my smart girl brain could not do anything but let the fun part of my brain start playing.

The other thing about an income intention is that this is who you are growing into. There is no date it has to be done by. You have created a big bubble and it will take you some time to grow into–and that is perfectly ok. What sounds more fun, an intention that you are going to grow into day by day, or a goal that you might not meet and get frustrated over?

Once I honored my income intention and started to grow into that bubble, my business followed. I more than doubled both my businesses in a year. Then I doubled my coaching business again in six months. At my current pace, it will double again in the next three months, and so on and so forth, which means in about six months I will be on pace to realize my original intention. In total, that will be about two years. I know for sure that if I had tried to just increase my income $10,000-$20,000 instead of setting the big intention, it would have taken me two years to do it, and I'm not sure I would have gotten there because the bubble would have been too small.

What is your income intention? The real one, not the one you adjusted with your smart girl brain, but the one that came from deep within your soul and your connection to your future self, the person you are more than capable of becoming?

Hold that number as sacred, because it is. And it will change your life.

Create Your Future Budget

Setting your sacred income intention is the first step. Now we're going to move on to how to deepen the experience. Close your eyes and imagine the target. The bullseye in the middle is the income, and when you set a *goal*, that is the only thing you focus on. It's your desired result, and there is little you think about outside of that except the steps to try and hit that bullseye. Anything outside of the center circle is close–but it's a miss.

What if the whole target was the bullseye? What if you cared about and got points for what was outside of the center circle? Would that make it easier to hit? How would that relieve the pressure of having to hit the bullseye, and make the process more fun?

Close your eyes and imagine the center circle is the income intention and everything around it is the life that surrounds that income. What surrounds it are the things you'll own, the experiences you will have, the feelings you will experience, and everything in between. It's your whole lifestyle.

Very often, when you set an income goal, you create a list of things that will come with that target, things you will buy like a new car, house, clothes, shoes. I remember, when I joined an MLM at 19, being taught to think of all the things I would have when I was making $100,000 a year. It was a want list, but the want list didn't tap into the experience of having those things or the emotional involvement. It was a list of stuff to attain, more or less, that was supposed to make me feel better. Only it didn't feel good to go after that list because it felt hollow. There was no depth to it, and honestly it didn't motivate me because what I actually wanted was a life and not a list of stuff. But no one taught me how to create an intention that included the life I wanted.

What I have learned that has made a big difference is, buying a car happens one time, on one day. The experience of driving that car, however, will happen over and over again. Getting the house you always dreamed of is amazing, but what you really want is the experience of living in that neighborhood and walking in to see the charm of the old door knobs every day, or stepping out to your favorite local restaurant. A list lacks depth and it keeps you just aiming at just the small circle in the middle, which for me lacked the connection to the life I actually wanted. If you can look at the list and extract the experiences you want to have, you can start building those experiences now. Then you are more likely to create the income you desire because you are creating a life instead of a list.

Understanding the depth of your intention is a key component to your determination to act in a way that leads you to your desired income. That is why next you are going to go through the process of creating your future budget. Yes, you will compile a list of ways to spend your money, and some of them will be on things. When you understand the list of things and how they fit together, you can begin to understand how your life will really be different and what the experiences are that will accompany your new income. By understanding the experiences, you can begin to step into them and live them now. It might sound crazy, but by stepping into them first, you will see the path to the income appear quicker and easier. Getting in touch with the experiences gets you in touch with your future self–and she is the one who knows the quickest path.

The truth most people miss is that living the life that your income intention allows you to live is the real prize. If the intention is $500,000, it is what that $500,000 will create that you really want. It's not $500,000 sitting in the bank just to say you did it. Those bragging rights are short-lived and likely not as fulfilling as turning the door to your home and taking off your shoes to walk on the original hardwoods. It's that solid, grand feeling when you come home that you desire, not a number you send your accountant at the end of the year. When you understand this difference, you realize there might not be one single roadmap to the magical experience you desire to be living.

The next step in the process is to look inside the life of your future self. There is a version of yourself in your future that is making the income you want to be making, and having the experiences that come with that life. You want to put yourself in her shoes and look around at her life to see what she is doing and what is happening. Most people will stand in the middle of their current reality and try and decide for their future self what she is doing, who she is being, and how she is living. You cannot know her from where you are right now. You must join her where she is, living that life you have been dreaming of, and see through the eyes of your future self. Of course, this is where we will engage the playful, creative side of your brain.

Going forward, I am going to refer to the person living your future life as your future self, but first, we have to satisfy the smart girl part of your current self. The smart girl part of your brain wants an understanding of what is going to be happening. When you make a list of "things" you are going to own with your new income, it doesn't give your smart girl brain enough information. While you may not consciously know it, she is frantically asking, "How do we know if this will be enough?" Or, "I don't know how we're going to spend all this money?" Or other questions like, "Who will want some if we have all this?"

The reason you don't know she is asking these questions is because she is scared and doesn't actually ask them out loud. Instead, she triggers freak-outs and what some might call self-sabotage. This is your smart girl brain's job. She cannot let you move forward without the answers. She cannot let you dream big and start moving in that direction if she does not know you will be safe when you get there. Whether you are making a lot or a little, too much or not enough, she knows how to manage your budget right now. It doesn't mean it's perfect, but she is operating with a set of rules and parameters that the two of you have unconsciously created, and before she can let you hop in the car for a road trip with a destination and no planned route, she needs to know the new rules of the road.

Here's how we are going to satisfy what your smart girl needs to know so that she can get on board. Put your sacred income intention in front of you. We are going to map out the financials of your future self.

If you are in your smart girl brain a lot, she is going to want to get hung up on taxes and things like that. Just put a number down for those things. She'll be ok. The less time you allow her to think about it, the less time she will have to analyze that stuff and will run with the answer you provide here. That said, take your income intention and do a quick Google search of tax brackets. Find the one your income intention would fall into, multiply your income intention by the tax bracket, and subtract that amount from your income intention. Yes, I know this will not be exact because things will change, you will have deductions, etc. That is ok. It will all work out. Any thoughts about the need for specificity are just the smart girl part of your brain trying to keep you safe, disguised as her being really smart and helpful. The quicker you do the math, the easier this will be.

For $500,000, I use 30%. I know that does not equate to the tax bracket, but it makes it easy and takes into account that there will be deductions etc. It will all work out just perfectly for this exercise. In reality, you are going to grow to this income over time, so you will be familiar with the tax amount and will have the money for it when you need it.

The next things I deduct are my business expenses. The smart girl will want you to go add up a bunch of things and do lots of calculations. Make it easy. You can estimate, which is what I do, about 20% after taxes—or you can get an actual percentage from your taxes for the previous year. Take your business deductions divided by your total business income, and use that percentage. Again, smart girl brain might say, "But my expenses will go up if I am making more money!" Here's the thing about the smart girl part of your brain. If you give her a number, like 20%, she will do a great job of keeping you within that range. If you tell her it's wide open, she won't know what to do and your expenses will likely grow because that is the story you are telling.

> For $500,000:
> After taxes, the amount remaining is $350,000
> After business expenses, the amount remaining is $280,000

If you were my client and $500,000 was your income intention, we would do the next part based on $280,000, or $23,333 a month. Calculate your number to move forward with. Then use it instead of $23,333, which I am going to use as an example going forward.

Now, allocate how your future self is investing (I never use the word spend because I think all money is an investment in something) $23,333 a month.

Just play with it first. Look at the number and see what your future self is doing with her money. What is your future self's mortgage or rent each month? What is your future self's car payment, if she has one? How much is your future self giving away to charity? Investing? Where is your future self traveling? What is your future self's travel budget for the year? What is your future self's investing money in ways she never thought would be possible? What is your future self doing that she loves?

Create your future budget from the middle of the life your future self is living. Close your eyes and imagine looking at your future self's bank statement and your future self's calendar. Don't do this based on what you "think" she will do. Really put yourself in your future self's shoes, and see how she is investing her money.

Allocate your future self's budget. Make sure you allocate every dollar of it. Many of my clients get to a point and go, well, then I'd put $10,000 in savings. Would your future self really be putting $10,000 in savings? And if so, what is that for? Often, the savings amount is at first based on your current self thinking about what you do not have. However, if you had $23,333 coming in every month, would you really be putting almost half of it into savings? My guess is no.

My client Allison and I were doing this exercise and she had $8,000 a month in savings at first. When I asked her what she was saving for, she had some good answers like, "Well, I'll need to save for things to do repairs to the house. I want to save some money for my kids. And I just want to have some there so I know it's there." All fine and good and seemingly very logical. That very logical-seeming part is coming from the smart girl part of your brain, and since this exercise is for your smart girl brain, then those answers should be fine, right? But they are actually coming from your current self asking what would you do with $23,333 right *now*, which means you aren't tapped into your future self. Your future self would know exactly where that money is going. At the end of one year, that would $120,000. At what point is there enough in the "just so I know the money is there" account?

If this is you, drill down further. With Allison, once we walked through it and I pointed out the $120,000 per year, she realized that was a lot to not actually have a plan for. I also explained to her that money is energy, and it likes direction. Money will flow to where there is a container for it. In this case, there really isn't a container, because it's mushy instead of solid to just label it "savings." Money is more likely to flow where the container is solid. Money really likes to be directed. The more you direct it, the quicker it will come. Take the time to get really clear about where all the money is going in your future life.

The other piece of this is becoming your future self. We are going to talk more about how getting to this income intention quickly and easily requires that you become the person who is making your income intention. Someone who is making $23,333 every month does not need to save $10,000 for "just in case," because next month another $23,333 is coming in. When you know money is coming over and over again, you behave differently. Really step into the place of making $23,333 a month.

I know your income isn't an exact amount every month. However, if you plan like it is, the range of income is likely to be less wide. Also, when you are consistently making $500,000 a year, you will allocate accordingly. If you expect that is what you are going to make, you will naturally save when months are a little higher and use the savings when they are a little lower. If your brain just told you to plan out the swing of income from one month to the next, that was actually your current self talking. Your current self is used to the swing, feast or famine, and does not trust the consistency. Your future self, the one making $500,000 a year, absolutely does.

The real reason people throw a lot of money into "savings" is because they do not know what else to do with it. Keep digging. Close your eyes and look over your future self's shoulder again. What does her life look like? What is the next trip she is going on? It feels easier to do this from the viewpoint of your current self, which is why you're tempted to put money into savings. But in order to truly know your future self, you have to know how she invests her money.

Now I am going to give you a second way to do this, rather than just putting down numbers. I do it both ways with my clients because they find more clarity doing both. One client said to me the following way felt more intentional than when he just wrote down how he would invest it.

The allocation I use is:
Living 60%
Fun 10%
Future 10%
Self-Growth 10%
Giving 10%

You can absolutely use any allocation method you would like. You can also adjust the percentages. It is just much easier when you have something to push against. When I did this exercise, here's how it went:

Living $14,000
Fun $2,333
Future $2,333

Self-Growth $2,333
Giving $2,333

Go through and allocate your income intention by percentage to get the dollar amount. Then take the dollar amount and break it down into exact amounts. In some cases, like travel, you will want to take your travel amount and multiple it by 12 to see what the total is. Then plan how you will invest that. Is it monthly weekend trips? Or a really big trip once a year and three or four little trips? Invest all the money. Actually look up the prices. Pick the charities you will be giving to. Allocate every cent of your income. The clearer you are about where the money will be invested, the quicker and easier the path to it will show up.

Chapter 4

Analyze Your Budget

The next step is to identify the experiences you are going to be having when you are making this income.

Usually the biggest expense people have is where they live, so start your future budget by allocating the amount you are going to invest in where you live. If this is a mortgage, Google a mortgage calculator so that you know what the price of that house would be. Then do a search of houses in that price range. Just because you allotted a certain amount for a mortgage does not mean you have to invest that. However if you find that you want to invest less, adjust the rest of your budget, and figure out where the extra money is going to be allocated. If you realize your budgeted amount does not afford you the house you really want, there are two things to do. The first one is to review the home you want. Is it really what you want? If the answer is yes, see where you can adjust your budget to allow it to work. If you want to rent your home, follow the same process and explore where you will be living. Even if you want to live in an RV, or be traveling and staying in multiple locations, figure out your home expenses.

When I did this exercise, I allocated $10,000 a month for a home. I actually decided that I wanted to rent. So, I started looking up what $10,000 a month in Denver opened the possibility to. What I found was magical to me. I was living in a building across the street from the Four Seasons Denver. The upper units have these massive balconies. Just a few years ago, I would look at those balconies and think to myself, "I would really love to live there, but that's just not in the cards." Even though I secretly really, really wanted to live there, I never admitted it. When I did my search of places to rent in Denver, the first thing that came up was one of the units at the Four Seasons with the huge balcony. I thought, that is definitely where my future self lives.

These are the types of possibilities that open up when you set your income intention and go through this process. The other thing that happens is that you see how your future self is different. One of my clients, Linda, said she would allocate a good portion of her budget to hosting parties. As we went through and clarified how much, we talked about what a party would be like. It included good friends, a good book discussion, a mixologist, a chef, and, of course, a party planner, because of course you need help with all that. I knew immediately this party was a big part of her future experience.

Look through your budget. Explore it for details and clues about the life your future self is living. Pick out three important experiences to take to the next step. Sometimes it's obvious, like the Four Seasons for me. With Linda, it was the intensity in her voice when she talked about the details of her party and, as we kept digging into that, this clued me into the fact that this is a major experience in her life.

Meet Your Future Self
Scripting

In order to complete the next step, which is to really get in touch with the experience of your future self's life, you need to pick out the three biggest highlights of your future life based on your future budget. For me, one of those highlights was living at the Four Seasons. As I mentioned, one of the highlights for Linda was throwing an amazing party. For another one of my clients, it was taking a dream trip to Antarctica. Each person's highlights are going to be different. They are unique to your future.

The best tool I have found for getting into your future self is scripting. The three highlights that you chose will be used for scripting. I developed a formula that puts you right into the heart of the experience:

Pick one of your experiences. Now put yourself in the middle of your future life, where that experience happens all the time. For example, if it were me, I would write about a day living at the Four Seasons. Most people would think you would want to write about moving in, but you actually want to write about being in the *middle* of your future life. Therefore, I would write about a regular Tuesday, living at the Four Seasons. For Linda, she would write about the day of the party because it is one special day that takes place in the middle of her amazing life. For my client whose future self goes to Antarctica, she will write about that experience.

The key to scripting is writing in the first person, *past tense*. The reason for this is that when you write in the present tense, your smart girl brain will argue that "that isn't true." However, when you use the past tense to write about all the amazingness in your life, you bypass your smart girl. Think of it this way: you are living your future life, with your future budget, and you are telling your best friend everything that happened the day before.

It might seem like it would be best to write about what is *going* to happen. If you do this, you are putting your intention out there–way out there. You are "wanting" it to happen and you could be "wanting" for a long time. Writing it as if it has already happened and you are already living that life, gets you in touch with the experience of your future self.

The true purpose of scripting is to get to know your future self inside her life. She is different than you, and getting to know her will give you the fast track to becoming her, which is the fastest track to your income intention. Writing as if you are already living that life by scripting in past tense gives you the inside track to who she is. Following the formula puts you even more in touch with who your future self is, how she feels, and what exactly is happening in her life. This is important for the next steps in the process.

Every script starts with waking up in the morning and falling asleep at night. Even if the highlight of your day is in the middle, start with waking up and what happens right up to that highlight event, and then continue to write about what "happened" after the event.

The formula for scripting is very important because it engages your senses, your emotions, and gratitude. Your senses and your emotions are key ways to get into the experience of your future self, and they allow you to start feeling who she is. Focusing on gratitude puts you in the place of appreciating what is happening in your future life. Note: gratitude, however, should be written in the *present* tense, because it is a present, ongoing, and key piece of manifestation. For some reason, your brain doesn't have a problem with that, so hard-wiring gratitude in the present tense makes it feel like it's already happening.

The formula is as follows:
Action: what you did next in your day
Sense: what you saw, heard, smelled, touched, tasted
Feeling: the emotion you felt–you want it to be positive and something you want to feel more of
Gratitude: being grateful for something in that moment

Here's an example:
I woke up. I listened to the birds chirping. I felt happy. I am so grateful I get to visit such an amazing place.

You will go step by step through your day following the formula for every detail and action that you do. This should take you a minimum of two hours, and is usually around two thousand words. If that sounds like a lot, that's because it is–you currently know very little about your future self. And the more you learn about who she is, the more you will realize how much more you need to get to know her. This method of tapping into everything gives you a very clear picture of your life so you can visualize it, and it automatically taps you into how it feels. It puts you in the experience. Go through all three days that you have selected based on your budget.

The place you might get off track is in the days you pick. Make sure these are based on your *future* budget, and not what you desire to happen next week.

When I was working through this process with my client Holly, we started talking about vacations. I asked her, based on her budget, where is her future self going? She told me Greece. I asked her if this was really her future self, the girl with the budget, where she would be going. She said that actually, she was going on a trip to Greece soon. Then we talked about all the other places she wants to go. I asked her, once you have been on vacation to all of your top places where are you going? Her answer was Hawaii. That is the vacation she should script, because it is the vacation her future self is taking. It's not that she is never going to Greece, but when she is making her income intention and she is in the middle of that life, she will have gone to Greece, probably multiple times, so she'll be ready to go to Hawaii.

I assigned Holly to script Hawaii and then next day when I read her script there was a note that she decided to do Greece instead. When we started talking through it, I asked her why she did it, and she realized she had decided to do it because it is what she wants next. It's ok to want what is next, but tapping into and scripting from the middle of the life of the person with your future budget will get you to your income intention faster, and it will also get you to Greece–your current want–faster. That is because the more you move into your future self, the faster things you desire will come to you in your current life.

Another example of a script that isn't your future self is something that talks about what you want next. It might sound something like this:

This morning I got my fifth client for the week. I saw the PayPal notice come through. I felt so happy. I am so grateful I just made $10,000.

The energy of that is all what you are trying to *make* happen, rather than being inside the life of your future self. One of the things I tell my clients about is: script the life, not the result. The life is everything that is happening when you have achieved your income intention. The result is the five clients you want now, or the things you think have to happen in order for you to get to your income intention.

Chapter 5

When you begin to start to experience the life your future self is living, the path to her life starts to appear quickly and easily. As you write, you will automatically discover more about who she is. The more you know about her, the more you can start to create her life. Then the more you create her life now, the quicker and easier your business grows.

Mirror Your Future Life

The first thing to do, now that you are in touch with your future self, is to go out and invest in something that makes a statement in your physical reality that your future self is there. It doesn't have to be something huge like redoing the whole house. It does not even have to cost a lot of money. It just needs be something your future self would have in her physical reality.

This is different for everyone. For my client Ana, it was a pad to put on her bed to make it even more comfortable, because her future self always wakes up rested. For some of my clients, it is as simple as a necklace that represents a place their future self has been. For Jana, it was a designer purse from the full price store instead of the outlet. For another client, it was bedding that made her feel like her future self. The key is that it comes out of the life of *your* future self.

Investing in something physical is like sticking the first stake in the ground where you are going to build a new house. It shows physically that the next steps are coming, the building of the house is inevitable. In your case, getting to your income intention is inevitable. Imagine being transported to a day in your future self's life. What would you bring back with you to remember being there?

Once you have set your income intention, created your future budget, and scripted your days, you will have a very good understanding of who your future self is and what to invest in should come to you without too much effort. If you need to just close your eyes and be quiet and still for a few minutes. Allow her to whisper the answer.

Returning to the target, you know that inside the center circle is your income intention, and you know the next ring is what your life experiences look like when you are making your income intention. The ring outside the experiences is the physical reality of your future life. That is the next ring you are going to focus on creating in the process of making the whole target the bullseye.

Your smart girl brain, as you know, is trying to protect you. Her job is to take the life you have said you are stepping into, and look around your life to see if it is true. When your brain looks at your physical reality–how are you behaving, what is physically in your life, and what you are doing– it starts to check if what you have said you wanted is coming true. If nothing has changed in the physical reality, your smart girl brain will sound the alarms because nothing seems different.

For instance, if, in your future life, your clothes will be more glamorous, but none of the clothes in your current closet are glamorous and you don't change that, your brain sees nothing is changing. If you want to hang out in cute yoga outfits, but you don't own any, your brain sees things as staying the same. Solving this problem can be as simple as cleaning the closet and putting something new that represents your future life front and center.

The same is true for furniture. If it looks different in your future, but you don't change anything now, your brain sees everything as the same. It doesn't mean you have to go buy all new things, but you could update the pillows on your couch, get a new couch cover, or add a fun table with a crazy decoration (if that's in your future life). Change some things in your environment so your brain knows things are changing.

If nothing changes, but you say you are going to make a big change, the alarms start sounding from your smart girl brain. These alarms do not sound like a fire truck or a tornado siren. You won't see the warning come across your TV. Instead they will show up as reasons you should not move forward. Really good reasons that you will believe. They will be really good reasons that totally make sense. Something inside will tell you that you need to slow down. The messages that this is not going to work will get very loud. Things will start happening in your life that seem like they are messages to stop, slow down, or change directions. You might also get sick.

All of these are actually ways that your system is trying to get you to step back into the old version of yourself and keep your income right where it is. These come up in part because you haven't changed your physical reality to match where you are headed. You have so much practice in the old reality that it feels comforting and familiar. Everything becomes routine. You see the same things. You do the same things. Something new in your reality will trigger your brain that things are changing.

After you have anchored your future self into your life, you are going to do an in-depth analysis of your current reality as compared to the reality you are living when you are making your income intention. Make a list of things that exist in your future self's life. Then highlight what is already true. Going forward, appreciate this as much as possible. You know that when a house appreciates, its value is growing. When you appreciate the things that already exist in your life that will also be in your future life, you are expanding those parts of your life.

After you start appreciating what already exists, you want to add in those things that do not exist yet as much as you can.

Stepping into Your Future

Once you have analyzed what is currently in your life and what isn't, you want to look for ways you can start stepping into the experiences you will have in your future life. For example, when I realized my future self was going to live at the Four Seasons Denver, I started looking at all the different options of places to live in the Four Seasons. Then I actually set up appointments to go look at them, because that is what I would be doing if I already had the income I was intending. I walked in not hoping or wishing I could live there, but telling the story to myself and everyone else that it was already in the process of it happening.

Another way to step into the experiences of your future self is to change the places you go. Give yourself more of the experiences you will be having in the future. If your new house will be in a new neighborhood you may want to shop at the neighborhood grocery store every so often. When I was intending to move to the Four Seasons, I would drive home as if I was living at the Four Seasons. I would get over into the lane I would use if I was going to turn in there to go home. I started to go to the spa at the Four Seasons so I was in the place I wanted to be. When I went in I acted like I lived upstairs. No one else knew what I was doing, but I did. There was a picture of a bedroom I wanted on my vision board that had a Buddha in it. So, when I found a small statue that looked like it, I bought it and I put it out. On that vision board was also a view I desired. It was two big windows looking at the mountains with a round pillar in the corner. When I moved into my new home, I realized that the exact view that was on my vision board–including the round pillar–is now the view in my living room.

Magical things start happening when you start stepping into the physical act of being your future self. My client Linda hadn't taken a vacation with her family in years. One thing she did when she was stepping into her future self was check out some vacation spots they wanted to go online. She was going on a vacation, and they were planning to stay at a cheap place, but she did what I tell my clients to do and practiced being the person with the money she will have in her future life. So, she checked out her dream place to stay. It just so happened that the day she was looking they were running an amazing special, so she booked it. They had a fabulous time and because she stepped right into it, she is even closer to her income intention. She also enjoyed the experience more.

One thing I suggest to my clients is to go have drinks and experience the restaurants where you will be eating in your future. If you do not have the money to eat there now, you can go in and enjoy a drink. Yes, it will cost more than having a drink somewhere else. It's an investment in your future life, and it will allow you to soak up the experience now. In addition to allowing you the experience now, it will give actual knowledge of what the restaurant looks and feels like so that your scripting will be deeper.

Another way to step into where you are going be living when you reach your income intention is to go to that neighborhood. Park your car and walk around as if you live there. Go to the coffee shop in that neighborhood. Start to step into the person who is living there. There are lots of ways to step into the future experiences you desire. Be creative and really put yourself inside that future you desire in order to figure out how to step into it.

Think of three ways you could start stepping into the experiences of your future self right now.

Feel Your Future

The outermost ring of the target is made up of the feelings you are going to feel inside your future life when your income intention is a reality. Traditional advice says to put off your life, work hard, and sacrifice now for what you desire later. The more you can feel now like you are going to feel when are making the income you desire, the quicker you will make the income. Suffering now will only push the income further out. You cannot become the person making that income quickly and easily if you are miserable, because miserable and easy don't normally go together.

Put yourself in the middle of your life earning your income intention. Look around and see all the experiences that come with your future budget and life. Now, name three feelings that describe that life. These are the feelings that you want to fill the majority of your life now. Take each feeling and ask yourself, "How can I feel more...." Write down the answers no matter how crazy they seem. Start to engage in them as often as possible.

You can also ask yourself, "Why don't I feel (insert your feelings)?" The answer that comes to you will give you clues about what might need to shift and change so that you can feel more of the feelings that will make up your future life.

When I did this exercise, the main feeling I came up with is "free." I started to ask myself, "Why don't I feel free?" When I started to explore why I wasn't feeling free, the answer I came up with is because there was no day where I could just do what I wanted. Sometimes I worked Saturday and Sunday. Sometimes I didn't. Often on Saturday and Sunday, there was something else I was committed to that didn't allow for a whole day to do what I wanted. I started taking Wednesdays off, and I felt so free. I credit taking Wednesdays off with figuring out exactly what I wanted to offer in my business and doubling my income.

Why did it matter if I took Wednesdays off? I was already not feeling free, which meant I really didn't feel like I had enough time for myself. The idea that changed my business is a four-day workshop where I take people step by step through this process, and they leave connected to their future self. Since I was already feeling like I had no free time, there is no way I was going to see the opportunity to take up my weekend days, which were only sometimes free. Taking Wednesdays completely off allowed me to see the possibility of the workshop, and teaching this process to people. If I hadn't activated the feeling of being free, which is what my $500,000 self feels like, I would have continued to struggle to figure out what the right path was.

Because our brains become accustomed to doing things and us living in a certain way, it's easy to slip back into old patterns. This happens to all of us, and it's normal. It doesn't mean you are doing it wrong. For example, a few months ago, I noticed I had loosened the boundary around Wednesdays. I noticed it first because I wasn't as happy in my business. Second, my income dropped. What

I realized is that by holding that boundary, I am being the person who makes $500,000. People are going to hire me because of the time I take for myself. My clients want to learn from someone who is taking care of themselves, and who feels good while pursuing their dreams. When I take Wednesdays off, I attract the right people. What kind of clients does your future self attract? Who is seeking her out to work with her? Becoming the person who is making your income intention is also about becoming the person your future clients want to hire and work with.

What Happens Next

When you start scripting based on the life you are living when you are making your income intention–making your life look like your future life, stepping into experiences, and finding ways to activate how you feel in your future life–magic starts happening. You will find that doors open that you couldn't get to open before. After working with me, Mia was able to get a condo she rents out on Airbnb to make money pretty much as soon as she landed back home from our weekend together. She had been trying to figure this out for months, but for one reason or another couldn't get it to come together. When she got in touch with and started stepping into her future self, the door opened immediately because making money easily was her future self. She is making so much that she has cut down to working just 25 hours a week. Her goal is to not have to work at all.

Another one of my clients, Cindy, scripted and started stepping into her future experiences. One of the things she wanted was the freedom to do the things she loves. She made time, when it seemed like she didn't have any, to invest in the things her future self would do. She was just gifted the ability to work from home. She works in sales, so she really only worked about two hours a day, but she had to go to work for six. Now, she works her two hours, and then goes and enjoys the freedom she now has. She is selling like crazy without working harder, because more and more people are just calling her. In fact the other day she told me how "easy" her sales have become.

Go Deeper

Keep scripting, and keep stepping into the experiences of your future self. Every time you do you get clearer about who she is and things will magically happen, just like with the two clients I just told you about. When those things happen, you get to experience her more and then you know her better. So when you script, it is deeper, and then you can step into her experiences on a deeper level, and then her experiences will show up more frequently, and the whole cycle just keeps repeating. Not only does it keep getting better and better, it also gets easier and easier.

How is your life going to feel when your business is easier?

Chapter 6

This process is magic. As I mentioned, it's helped me double my business three times in the last eighteen months, and I watch it work over and over again with my clients. The problem is that it is not something you have known all your life. It is new and fresh, and I want to make you aware of a couple places where you might get off track and a few things that can happen in the process even if you are following the formula. I want you to be successful so it's important to highlight these things so you can recognize them and ask for help if you need it.

The first way you can get off track is by not setting a high enough income intention. This happens when people follow the process and get a really big number, then decide there is no way they could do that, or that it will be better if they just go slower. It won't. I promise you. I can tell when my clients are not telling the truth about the number that comes to them. This happened with my client Sarah. I could tell when she told me the number that she had changed it a bit. I coached her to tell me what really came to her, and she did. The information that opened because we used the real number is making all the difference in her getting where she wants to be. Had we used a number that was not accurate, her budget would have been off and then her scripting and everything else would have been off, too.

Additionally, if you create from a space where you have stepped back because you are scared, you are creating from a place of fear, which usually creates scarcity. It's the opposite of what you desire. Own that the number you get is likely going to be scary. Of course it is. You don't know what it is like to be a person who makes that much. Your brain is just doing its job by making you a little afraid and asking, "Are you sure?" Say, "Yes," claim the bigness, and start stepping into it.

Another way you could get derailed is by not scripting from the place of your future budget. Recently, one of my clients, Candice, switched up what she was scripting about. When we were going through some other things, I asked her why she made the switch. Candice said it was because this particular day is closer to her current life and she wanted to know it was happening, meaning she was going to get where she wanted. The problem with this is Candice wasn't scripting from her future self. She was scripting from her current self. She was trying to make things happen by scripting about the thing she wanted to happen now, like more clients. This was actually keeping her from growing into the person who has more clients.

It's easy to think that if I script the life I have now and just add in what I want it, will happen faster. Unfortunately, it doesn't–because that is keeping your bubble small, like we talked about earlier in the book, and it doesn't allow you to grow in the way you need to in order for the path to your desired business to show up. Since Candice and I looked at what she was doing and adjusted it to make sure she's keeping her bubble big and scripting from the place of her future self, instead of trying to control the outcome, her business had taken off in lots of ways.

Scripting is the process for getting in touch with your future self. It's how you get into her psyche. It's how you learn to understand her. It's how you get familiar with your future life. Once you know her you start to take stock of the experiences you are having that resemble her life. Scripting what feels easier is trying to make something happen faster. Your job is not to make anything happen faster. It's to get in touch with her and her life and make your life as closely resemble that as possible. In general you want to script the thing that feels the farthest away. That will give you the most insight on what is going to be different so that you can start connecting with those experiences. It can be easy to step back, like Candice did, because you want it to happen faster. Check in with yourself and your scripting to make sure you are staying in the bigness, because that is what is going to get you there the quickest and easiest way possible.

After you read this book and do the process, you are going to want your income intention to come true so badly–because now you know how really good it is to live that life. Something is likely to come up that makes you think it's the magic pill to that life. By magic pill, I mean the quick way. This will look like it's a direct path, but it is really putting you on the quick, slow path.

That's what happened to my client Holly after she finished her three days with me. She is such a good student, and dove right into what she was supposed to do. Then up popped a course that she almost got sucked into. This course was about getting more clients. She said her future self would know how to get more clients and that is the reason she was thinking about it. Because she works with me, I was able to spot it right away. We talked through it and she realized it was a quick path idea and not her future self coming through.

One of my other clients, Linda, explained how when she started, she had lots of ideas about things she needed to do. Each time one of these came up, we would discuss it, and I would remind her to tap into her future self for the answer. There was not one additional thing she found she needed to do, and the more she went through the process and stepped into her future self, the more she felt like she just became her future self. She did not have to study or force it. She simply followed the process and her inspiration. Then, more and more of what she wants just shows up for her.

This happens to almost everyone who takes my course, so just be aware it's likely to happen to you. When it does—before you buy or invest in anything—get quiet and really check into what it feels like. How does the energy around it feel? When inspiration is coming from your future self, it feels calm, inevitable, like just the next step. When it's your current self wanting to get there as quickly as possible, it feels rushed, like it's the only option, like you have to do it or you won't get where you are going. These are really good feelings to be on the lookout for after completing the process. It will help you stick with the process and avoid going back to the slow, quick path.

Another thing that might happen if you just read this book is that you won't do the whole process. Completing the whole process is very important. When you start the process, you are really opening up the channels to your income intention. Following the process allows your brain to stay with you and not freak out. Doing half of the process can actually put you further behind, because your brain can start feeling pressured to keep you safe and small when you haven't given it all the information. When that happens, it's easy to do something to self-sabotage. When your smart girl brain has proof this was too big, too fast and it's not working, she will work twice as hard to keep you safe, which is why something that looks like self-sabotage might happen. The way to avoid this is to go all in, or not start the process at all. Make a choice and follow through with it. Either choice is perfect, by the way.

Honestly, this process can be scary. We are not talking about an extra $10,000-$20,000 here. We are talking about creating an income that truly supports your happiness and what you want to be doing with your time, energy, and life. Setting your income intention is not about money, it's about your life and your happiness. Those are sacred and should be treated as such. Honor the sacred. Honor that stepping into your future life probably requires you to step up in ways that you did not see coming. It might actually seem easier at one point to just mail out more flyers or something similar. The way to avoid getting off track and sticking to the process so that you have the life you desire is to make the commitment right now to you, your life, and your dreams that you are worth going all in–and then honor that commitment.

I love reading books but I get more out of one-on-one interaction. If you find yourself loving the process in this book, but getting stuck, I am always happy to go deeper with you.

You can go to http://www.imreadytodoublemybusiness.com *and schedule a call with me.*

Chapter 7

One client can change everything. If I were coaching Kerri, the real estate agent I mentioned at the beginning of the book, I would tell her I am that one client for my realtor. I walked into an open house he was doing. I had a realtor, and I wasn't actually in the market for a new property. I was a nosy neighbor who wanted to see the condo where he was holding an open house.

Six months later, we ended up working together—and not because he sent me a calendar every month or called me every eight weeks. I ended up being his client because he was being the realtor who was making his future income, and he followed his intuition. His intuition said to send me an email one day about a specific property, and he did. He wasn't grabby or desperate. He was just serving and being the person who was making his next income level. As a client, I more than doubled his business. He made more from working with me than he had his whole first year in real estate, which was over $30,000. That doesn't include the almost $20,000 he has made working with my sister, and the additional $6,000 he will make when we close on my next property.

Incidentally, that realtor went on to take my Double Your Business course, and he just reached out today, as I am writing this, to tell me that everything had changed for the better since. He'd actually had a slower month than usual, but because he'd taken the course, he had total faith and zero stress–he knew the money would show up. He has seven closings scheduled for the next month, and, since the condo I am selling (not where I'm currently living) is about to go under contract, he will probably have eight. He said something very important: "We have always lived abundantly, but I was always scared when we did it. Now, I do it and I enjoy it."

He's moved his plan to relocate to another state up by a couple years too. Since working with me, he was also able to buy half of his family cabin, so it didn't have to be sold and he could have it to share with his kids.

I was talking to an inspector at one my places, and he told me he was taking the real estate license exam. He then went on to tell me that he doesn't have a market because he moved to Denver from out of town. It's a very traditional belief that your network is what is going to determine your success or failure. I explained to him about how my realtor and I met. Traditional wisdom says it's who you know that will make the difference in your business. The truth is it is who you are *being* that will help you create the life you want, and a byproduct of that is a successful business.

The choice you have before you is: do you want to be someone who does more marketing because it is the thing to do, or do you want to step into the version of yourself who has the income she desires and watch the path magically unfold in front of her? Make no mistake, I am not saying the latter will be easy. But it will be quicker, easier and filled with fun and joy.

What will it feel like to wake up in five years more alive and happier than you have ever felt? What will it feel like to come home and open the door to turn-of-the-century charm with modern-day luxury? What will it feel like to spend a week in Tuscany drinking wine and watching the sunflowers turn toward the sun? What will it feel like to be making the impact you want to make, and to love the business you have built? All this is my wish for you. Set your income intention and start becoming that woman, or man, today, so that tomorrow the answers, the clients, and the houses find you.

You are worthy of the life you've always dreamed of, and a business that supports you being able to create that in a way that feels easy and really good. You have always worked hard to achieve your goals, and this time is no different. I know you will get there one way or another. That's who you are. It's what you do.

For some people, reading this book is enough. It will change everything. One of my readers of my last book, *Manifest $10,000*, was able to immediately put everything into practice that I teach in that book and manifest $7500 in the twenty-four hours after she finished reading it. My hope for all my books is that someone will pick them up, read, do everything, and experience the success I know is waiting for them.

For others, they take a piece of the book that made a difference to them and integrate it into their lives. It becomes part of their life, and they experience a small up level because they took a part of what I said to heart.

Then there is the group that I used to find myself in, and that is the people who read the book and try to implement it on their own. They don't get the results they wanted, and end up feeling bad and possibly even more stuck than before. Make the commitment to yourself right now to get the help you need. I often get on the phone with people who read one of my books six months ago and think they are doing everything right, but are not getting the results. Within minutes of talking to them, I can pinpoint the major point they missed or overlooked that will change their results.

Whatever you do, don't suffer. If you get stuck, seek help. If you get frustrated, find a cheerleader. I love the transformations I am able to guide my clients through, and I am always open to going deeper. If it's not me, find a coach who resonates to support you through the process.

This is not just about another sale or another client. It's not even about doubling your business. This is about your life. You have the power to design the life and business you want, and have it manifest around you quicker and easier than you ever thought possible. Set your income intention, follow the steps to make it a reality, and do whatever it takes. Because you are worth living the best story you can tell.

Bonus Chapter:

Read This One First

Thank you so much for purchasing this book. I know you are committed to doubling your business without doubling your hours so that you can actually enjoy the life you have built, and I want to make success as inevitable as possible. So I created a few things to support your journey:

- An audio version of this book available at DoubleYourBusinessBook.com

- A season on the *Happy Ever After* Podcast that compliments this book. You can check it out on iTunes, episodes 27-39. Click here to listen.
- A complimentary four-part video course, *How to Double Your Business Without Doubling Your Hours*. Register at DoubleYourBusinessBook.com

About the Author

Cassie Parks is a Lifestyle Design Strategist. She is a real estate investor, champagne lover, coach, and guide for those who want to step into the life of their dreams.

After creating the ability to "retire at 32" from her real estate investments, she set out to use the same principles to build a coaching practice that she loves and affords her both the time and income for lifestyle she desires to live.

She lives floating amidst the Denver skyline. When she's not traveling, she can be found enjoying the pool in the middle of the workday, taking care of herself in the spa, or laughing with friends on her balcony.

Cassie works closely with two business owners a month who want to double their business. To find our more go to http://www.liveyourchampagnelife.com/work-with-cassie/

Cassie's introductory program is *Manifest $10,000*, and is open to anyone who is ready to welcome more money into their lives.

You can hear more about Doubling Your Business on the Happy Ever After show. Available on iTunes.

Thank You

Are you ready to double your business without doubling your hours so that you can actually enjoy the life that you have built?

I want to sincerely thank you for purchasing this book. I had no idea as I started down my journey with this process that one day I would be teaching it to others. Your life, your income, and your business are things I consider sacred, and I appreciate you inviting me along on your journey.

As a thank you, I have created some things to support your journey.

First:

- A free audio version of this book
- A free video course

Both of these are available at DoubleYourBusinessBook. com

And:

- A season (episodes 27-39) of the Happy Ever After podcast dedicated to this process. You can listen on iTunes here.

Of course if you read this book and you know this is the way to double your business quickly and easily, but you know you want and need support along the journey, you can apply to work with me at http://www. imreadytodoublemybusiness.com

Morgan James
Speakers Group

www.TheMorganJamesSpeakersGroup.com

We connect Morgan James published authors with live and online events and audiences whom will benefit from their expertise.

Morgan James makes all of our titles available
through the Library for All Charity Organization.

www.LibraryForAll.org

Printed in the USA
CPSIA information can be obtained
at www.ICGtesting.com
JSHW080004150824
68134JS00021B/2265